BLOODAXE WORLD POETS · 5

NAOMI SHIHAB NYE
TENDER SPOT

BLOODAXE WORLD POETS

An international series of vital voices in world poetry, all speaking to the general reader as well as to the poetry lover – major modern writers from *Staying Alive* and its companion anthologies.

Further titles in the series to be announced.

STAYING ALIVE SERIES

Neil Astley's international anthologies introduce new readers to contemporary poetry, with thematic selections of thoughtful and passionate poems about living in the modern world. They give existing poetry readers a much wider range of contemporary poems than other modern anthologies, including work by many poets even the keenest readers will be surprised to discover.

BLOODAXE WORLD POETS · 5

NAOMI SHIHAB NYE

Tender Spot

SELECTED POEMS

BLOODAXE BOOKS

ISBN: 978 1 85224 791 1

First published 2008 by
Bloodaxe Books Ltd,
Highgreen,
Tarset,
Northumberland NE48 1RP.

www.bloodaxebooks.com
For further information about Bloodaxe titles
please visit our website or write to
the above address for a catalogue.

Bloodaxe Books Ltd acknowledges
the financial assistance of
Arts Council England, North East.

Cover design: Neil Astley & Pamela Robertson-Pearce.

Cover printing: J. Thomson Colour Printers Ltd, Glasgow.

Printed in Great Britain by
Bell & Bain Limited, Glasgow, Scotland.

In memory of my father, Aziz Shihab
1927-2007

I spoke to the land and said, 'Please remember me
and take care of my tear trees and remember that others
may covet you and try to own you but you will always
be mine.' I threw kisses toward the earth.

Does the Land Remember Me? A Memoir of Palestine (2007)

ACKNOWLEDGEMENTS

The poems in this selection are drawn from these books by Naomi Shihab Nye: *Words Under the Words: Selected Poems* (Far Corner Books, 1994), *Red Suitcase* (BOA Editions, 1994), *Fuel* (BOA Editions, 1998), *19 Varieties of Gazelle: Poems of the Middle East* (Greenwillow Books / HarperCollins, 2002) and *You & Yours* (BOA Editions, 2005).

'A Big Life' is reprinted from *Contemporary Poets*, 7th edition, ed. Thomas Riggs (St James Press, 2001). 'Loose Leaf' is reprinted from *Words Under the Words*.

Acknowledgements are due to the editors of the following publications in which some of the new poems first appeared: *Court Green, Five Points, Midwest Quarterly, Tikkun*, and *We Begin Here: Poems for Palestine and Lebanon*, edited by Kamal Boullata and Kathy Engel (Interlink, 2007). 'Parents of Murdered Palestinian Boy Donate His Organs to Israelis' was published on a broadside from Pyramid Atlantic Art Center.

CONTENTS

from YOU AND YOURS (2005)

NEW POEMS (2008)

A BIG LIFE

We go back to where it all begins. The sources, the mysterious wells. Each thing gives us something else.

It was not whether you were rich or poor, but if you had a big life, that was what mattered. A big life could be either a wide one or a deep one. It held countless possible corners and conversations. A big life did not stop at the alley or even the next street. It came from somewhere else and was going somewhere, but the word 'better' had no relation really. A big life was interested and wore questions easily. A big life never thought for one second it was the only life.

Something was in the closet, besides our clothes, which might or might not be friendly. A branch scratched a curious rhythm on the dark window. Our father came from Palestine, a beloved land, far across the sea. Some people called it the Holy Land. Both my parents seemed holy to me. At night our father sat by our beds, curling funny stories into the air. His musical talking stitched us to places we had not been yet. And our mother, who had grown up in St Louis, where we were growing up, stood by our beds after our father's stories, floating into sleep on a river of songs: 'Now rest beneath night's shadow...' She had been to art school and knew how to paint people the way they looked on the inside, not just the outside. That is what I wanted to know about too. What stories and secrets did people carry with them? What songs did they hold close in their ears?

Reading cracked the universe wide open; suddenly, we had the power to understand newspapers, menus, books. I loved old signs, Margaret Wise Brown, Louisa May Alcott, Carl Sandburg, Langston Hughes, the exuberant bounce of sentences across a page. I remember shaping a single word – 'city', 'head' – with enormous tenderness. In second grade my class memorised William Blake's *Songs of Innocence*. Reading gave us voices of friends speaking from everywhere, so it followed that one might write down messages too. Already I wrote to find out what I knew and what connected. Sometimes writing felt like a thank-you note, a response to what had already been given.

My German-American grandmother gave me a powder puff that, when tapped thirty years later, still emits a small, mysterious cloud.

My Palestinian grandmother gave me a laugh and a tilt of the head.

My great-uncle Paul gave me a complete sewing-kit a hundred years old and one inch tall.

Whenever people have asked, 'Where do you get ideas to write about?" I wonder, 'Where do you not?'

NAOMI SHIHAB NYE

LOOSE LEAF

I was thumbing through a childhood picture album, its vintage red cover embossed with the golden word PHOTOGRAPHS, wondering exactly when and how all the pages let go of one another. They were still stacked, but no longer chronological or bound at the seam. I used to dream of having a loose-leaf file.

Here I am wearing a polka-dotted headscarf, soberly pushing a stuffed rabbit in a baby carriage. Preparing to blow out two candles on a cake. Holding and being held. With neighbors who disappeared into the world and were never seen by us again. With baby brother freshly home from the hospital. With grandparents who died. With the cat that froze in the snow one winter. We tried to thaw him out in a warm oven. The underpants, the shutters, the wooden bedframes, the plump 1950s sofas. Here are the friendly immigrants who frequented our address and the concrete steps everybody fell down and the trees that may or may not still be rooted in the deep, silent ground. I wore a party dress and stood grinning with my legs crossed like an X. Immediately after that picture was taken, I fell over and hit my head on the fence. It was the first time I realised how a day could change.

I think of the invisible pictures between the pictures, and under them. What was said that made us all look that way at just that moment? The gleam of particulars. My life, anybody's life. I've looked at albums belonging to people I barely know and could swear I recognised people in their photographs. Isn't that what happens with poems? When we let that luckiness come in.

In one scene my sleek-skinned shirtless father and I are digging in a garden with pitchforks. Our soil looks lumpy and dry, clotted with weeds and grass. Behind us our neighbor's tomatoes stand neatly tied to poles, head-high. We must have been slow that year. 'What did we ever plant?' my father asks, forty springs later, staring hard at the photograph.

'Tomatoes,' I say. 'We must have planted tomatoes too. Let's ask Mom. She'll remember.'

The mystery of remembering has added its own light to the

garden. Whatever existed then has deepened, been forgotten or restored in some other form. We planted our voices. We planted the things we feared and hoped they'd go away. We ourselves were going away, but each day felt like a whole world, rich and round and thick with dreams. Where are all those days no one took a picture of? Maybe they're in your album.

NAOMI SHIHAB NYE

TOUCHING TENDER SPOTS

1

The poems in *Tender Spot* touch many, diverse tender spots. Whether singing a lullaby for a child or praising simplicity in wise elders, while visiting far-flung places or imagined destinations, Naomi Shihab Nye feels at home with all peaceful beings. When writing about the Palestine of her father (Aziz Shihab, author of *Does the Land Remember Me?* and *A Taste of Palestine*) and about the Middle East in general, we also hear her ethical conscience questioning 'authority' with stinging critiques.

But Shihab Nye does not speak for voiceless 'Arabs' in *Tender Spot* – just as John Howard Griffin did not speak for segregated 'Negroes' in *Black Like Me* (1961). Their narratives map a reality of oppression and record authentic idioms of pain. Griffin was a humanitarian who clarified the cultural patterns of racism and battled injustice. Today we call such individuals human rights activists. Yet the universal principles of prejudice never change, even while bad actors rehearse indefensible rationalisations. How ironic that becoming a human rights activist, which she does not label herself, demands only one simple prerequisite – that we act humanely toward humanity beyond mere self-interest.

Since her earliest published work, Shihab Nye has composed elegies and homages for individuals around the world and meditative lyrics of home life. Yet the domestic poems are never domesticated and the travel poems are never foreign. False dichotomies of domestic or foreign, of high or low culture, of evil guerilla terrorism v. benign state terrorism – or of claiming intrinsic differences between Self and *Other* – become resolved in that rare dimension we might call spiritual empathy.

2

One of Shihab Nye's ways of awakening readers has been to narrate from a child's viewpoint, forcing adults to encounter innocence again. These children ask questions adults do not ask, nor want asked of them – valid queries that illuminate the absurdity of powerful nations waging war for stolen territory, natural resources and profit, while always exacting the price of 'collateral damage' paid in blood by innocent civilians. She writes of those living under occupation, but also about students and kids on the streets of America; in addition, there are poems about her son growing up and of her own childhood memories. (Her books for children and young adults tend not to confront brutal horrors, but nonetheless are concerned with moral imperatives.)

There are several poems about children at risk in her recent collection, *You & Yours* (2005).

'For Mohammed Zeid of Gaza, Age 15' detects a linguistic fault line beneath a crime: 'There is no stray bullet, sirs' / 'So don't gentle it, please.' Unlike Mohammed, 'this bullet had no innocence, did not / wish anyone well, you can't tell us otherwise / by naming it mildly, this bullet was never the friend / of life, should not be granted immunity / by soft saying – friendly fire, straying death-eye, / why have we given the wrong weight to what we do?' Surely "authorities" of all stripes would dismiss these concerns as naïve.

In 'The Day' a voice wonders if 'I missed the day / on which it was said / others should not have / certain weapons, but we could. / Not only could, but should, / and do.' Perhaps she had missed that day, 'Or maybe I wasn't born yet.' Such truths have deadly consequences, but are rarely debated in the corporate media. But 'What about the other people / who aren't born? / Who will tell them?'

3

'The Light that Shines on Us Now' confronts the arrogance of 'This strange beam of being right, / smug spotlight.' A 'little one' asks: 'What else could we have done?' An adult voice declares: 'Now that we are so bold, / now that we pretend / God likes some kinds of killing, / how will we deserve / the light of candles, / soft beam of a small lamp / falling across any safe bed?' That safety we once took for granted has become a nightmare of "foreign" terrorism amid the bellicose color-coded warnings.

'During a War' begins at the end of a friend's letter: '*Best wishes to you & yours,*' wondering, 'where does "yours" end?' while implying *where does mine begin?* It ponders the tragedies in the Middle East that military occupiers have defensively denied or sanctimoniously dismissed. 'Your family, / your community, / circle of earth, we did not want, / we tried to stop, / we were not heard / by dark eyes who are dying / now.' This "letter" laments what war profiteers and spy agencies generally cheer in secrecy. Yet 'How easily they / would have welcomed us in / for coffee, serving it / in a simple room / with a radiant rug. / Your friends & mine.'

How far away from American shores violence seemed before 9/11 – or, at least, easier to ignore. Since then any word by Shihab Nye concerning the Middle East – once reviewed as literature of "cultural enrichment" – has sometimes been judged to be faintly unpatriotic by far-right pundits. Yet by traveling extensively (and often with her husband, the brilliant documentary photographer Michael Nye), she has consistently connected on the human level with a vast circle of witnesses in war-torn areas – watching, listening, transmitting their stories and poems into several anthologies, as well as in her own collections of poetry.

4

While even her earliest work focused on the culture and people of Palestine – especially tender poems about her father and paternal grandmother – most texts are not overtly political. Certainly she never intended to be a 'political poet' and has never slipped into ideology. In fact, she flatly declares in the first stanza 'Jerusalem' that 'I'm not interested in / who suffered the most. / I'm interested in / people getting over it,' realising that peace will never arrive at the sites of oppression and revenge.

In the second stanza, she relates a charming anecdote told by her father, which shifts from the bold statement opening 'Jerusalem': 'Once when my father was a boy / a stone hit him on the head. / Hair would never grow there. / Our fingers found the tender spot / and its riddle: the boy who has fallen stands up.' Then she expands the anecdote into a larger context of relative experience. 'Each carries a tender spot: something our lives forgot to give us.' There we have the source of her title, although implied 'tender spots' are touched throughout these selected poems. Near the end of this poem, she returns to say:

'There's a place in this brain / where hate won't grow. / I touch its riddle: wind, and seeds.'

In her earlier books – *Different Ways to Pray*, *Hugging the Jukebox*, *Yellow Glove* and *Red Suitcase* – there are humorous takes on American social habits, light-hearted narratives on local characters, and subtle personal meditations reflecting shades of emotion that have nothing to do with politics. These are the books for which she became known nationally as a poet, containing work that evokes the little unnoticed mysteries of daily existence with a freshness of perception.

5

In almost every text – be it lyric or narrative or prose poem – there nests a vulnerable image at the heart of poetry. 'Fresh' observes a moment when nothing seems to be happening: 'To move / cleanly. / Needing to be / nowhere else. / Wanting nothing / from any store. / To lift something / you already had / and set it down in / a new place. / Awakened eye / seeing freshly. / What does that do to / the old blood moving through / its channels?' It moves mountains when immersed in the eternal moment, even if only a pot plant or curio has taken up new residence on the same shelf.

This awareness of Being in solitude becomes the encounter with Poetry. Over and over, she turns non-events at home into splendid, compressed lyrics. 'Open House' confesses to 'work as hard as I can / to have nothing to do. // Birds climb their rich ladder of choruses.// They have tasted the top of the tree, but they are not staying.// The whole sky says, Your move.' Open house, indeed with eyes on the sky.

The simple language belies these witty epiphanies. Even in a much earlier poem ('Adios') we realise that variations on 'the small alphabet of departure' are saying goodbye once the words reach print. 'Explain little, the word explains itself. / Later perhaps. Lessons following lessons, / like silence following sound.' Always a pure sound or whisper on the lips of silence. 'Eye Test' plays with a more fragmented alphabet – beginning with a stanza that puns on letters, then a stanza expressing enthusiasm for stories over eye charts: 'How much better to be a story, story. / Can you read me?' Even in such brief poems there are outlines of a story beneath, and also a continued delight in the art of telling stories – a reaching back to nomadic cultures that were the earliest source of folk entertainment provided by her father.

6

While there may not be a prototypical text in the academic sense, we do hear a similar ironic tone and sense a serious playfulness at work, befitting a renegade voice. 'Fuel' typifies this irony, suggesting things are not as they may seem. 'Once my teacher set me on a high stool / for laughing. She thought the eyes / of my classmates would whittle me to size. / But they said otherwise.' The eyes, mind you, not her classmates, while our laughing student escapes the intended effect of her punishment: 'I pinned my gaze out the window / on a ripe line of sky. // That's where I was going.'

'One Boy Told Me' strings a series of remarks over time – made by her son, Madison, a childlike renegade – composed as declarations and retorts. 'Music lives inside my legs,' he declares. 'It's coming out when I talk.' Later, a fresh observation as a rebuke: 'Grown-ups keep their feet on the ground / when they swing. I hate that.' Parents, even the gently understanding, still stand as authority figures. 'Don't talk big to me,' he warns. 'I'm carrying my box of faces. If I want to change faces I will.' Child as shape-shifter in a defiant dance of masks. 'When I grow up my old names / will live in the house where I live now. / I'll come and visit them.' The charming rant ends: 'It is hard being a person.//I do and don't love you – / isn't that happiness?'

Experience, then, becomes the real authority, from childhood challenges to the ledge of learning to examine ourselves. In 'Living With Mistakes' she personifies her own wet mistakes with a dry wit. 'They won't wear boots. / They march ahead of us / into our rooms, dripping. // Give them a chair. / Where they sit, / the fabric will be wet / for days.' Not only wet, but staring disdainfully with authoritative eyes: 'We have to talk about everything else / in their presence.'

7

In 'Always Bring a Pencil' we hear a teacher's voice assuring us that 'There will not be a test.' Erasing the tension of unknowing

18

with the soft end of the pencil, she tenderly warns: 'But there will be certain things – / the quiet flush of waves, / ripe scent of fish, / smooth ripple of the wind's second name – / that prefer to be written about / in pencil.' A pointed lesson in creativity – but why a pencil? Well, because 'It gives them more room to move around.' Therefore, a sensorium at the threshold of naked experience – primal waves, ancient scents, wind as naming music – all in free motion, touching tender spots connected by undivided attention in an object lesson.

We find another lesson of naming hidden in 'Hidden' – one perhaps for adults, who need to be attentive to the meaning. 'If you place a fern / under a stone,' it begins, 'the next day it will be / nearly invisible / as if the stone has swallowed it.' The parallel second stanza moves around inside you. 'If you tuck the name of a loved one / under your tongue too long / without speaking it / it becomes blood / sigh / the little sucked-in breath of air / hiding everywhere / beneath your words.' Eventually a fern shall emerge as it reaches for the light, and the name will be called out from under words. 'Hidden' ends with a rush that awakens the old blood: 'No one sees / the fuel that feeds you.'

We cannot lose the intense focus so essential in desperate times. Truthfulness has revealed the lies of governments which have made us blind accomplices to senseless destruction. Once aware of our complicity, we must try to heal the wounds of violence and injustice in order to become more than guilty bystanders.

8

Finally, we return to the beginning, to that encounter with poetry.

The great voice of 'Paul Robeson stood / on the northern border of the USA / and sang into Canada...' And not only that, across the border listened 40,000 Canadians! Let us say that 'His voice left the USA / when his body was / not allowed to cross / that line.' What line in the sand? Sovereign demarcations at imaginary borders and walls of separation imposing ghettos of segregation? 'Remind us again, brave friend. / What countries may we not sing into?'

This suggests a declension of inquiry: What countries may I not think about, what places may you not love, what home may

19

he or she not defend peacefully, 'What lines should we all be crossing?' – and where are they when we need to be human? However, there stands the last question of 'Cross that Line': 'What songs travel toward us / from far away / to deepen our days?'

Songs like these, the lucid poems of Naomi Shihab Nye, touching tender spots across every line.

ROBERT BONAZZI

Robert Bonazzi's publications include the critically-acclaimed *Man in the Mirror: John Howard Griffin and the Story of Black Like Me,* and four books of poetry, most recently, *Maestro of Solitude: Poems & Poetics* (Wings Press, 2007). His authorised Estate editions of *Black Like Me* (Wings Press, 2006) and *Man in the Mirror* (Orbis, 1997) remain in print. He writes a column, *Poetic Diversity*, for the *San Antonio Express-News*.

from

DIFFERENT WAYS
TO PRAY

(1980)

Minnows

All night I stare into the mirror
at the deep wrinkle beginning to show
on my forehead above the right eye.

I move the muscles of my face
to see where it comes from
and it comes from everywhere,
pain, joy, the look of being puzzled
and raising one eyebrow,
from the way I say YES too much,
I say YES when I mean NO
and the wrinkle grows.

It is cutting a line across my head
like a crack in a creek bottom –
starting small, shiver between two stones,
it ends up splitting the bed.

I wade carefully, feeling with feet –
smooth-skinned pebbles,
the minnow's effortless glide.

The Art of Disappearing

When they say Don't I know you?
say no.

When they invite you to the party
remember what parties are like
before answering.
Someone telling you in a loud voice
they once wrote a poem.
Greasy sausage balls on a paper plate.
Then reply.

If they say We should get together
say why?

It's not that you don't love them any more.
You're trying to remember something
too important to forget.
Trees. The monastery bell at twilight.
Tell them you have a new project.
It will never be finished.

When someone recognises you in a grocery store
nod briefly and become a cabbage.
When someone you haven't seen in ten years
appears at the door,
don't start singing him all your new songs.
You will never catch up.

Walk around feeling like a leaf.
Know you could tumble any second.
Then decide what to do with your time.

Kindness

Before you know what kindness really is
you must lose things,
feel the future dissolve in a moment
like salt in a weakened broth.
What you held in your hand,
what you counted and carefully saved,
all this must go so you know
how desolate the landscape can be
between the regions of kindness.
How you ride and ride
thinking the bus will never stop,
the passengers eating maize and chicken
will stare out the window forever.

Before you learn the tender gravity of kindness,
you must travel where the Indian in a white poncho
lies dead by the side of the road.
You must see how this could be you,
how he too was someone
who journeyed through the night with plans
and the simple breath that kept him alive.

Before you know kindness as the deepest thing inside,
you must know sorrow as the other deepest thing.
You must wake up with sorrow.
You must speak to it till your voice
catches the thread of all sorrows
and you see the size of the cloth.

Then it is only kindness that makes sense anymore,
only kindness that ties your shoes
and sends you out into the day to mail letters and purchase
bread,
only kindness that raises its head
from the crowd of the world to say

It is I you have been looking for,
and then goes with you everywhere
like a shadow or a friend.

Colombia

Walking Down Blanco Road at Midnight

There is a folding into the self which occurs
when the lights are small on the horizon
and no light is shining into the face.

It happens in a quiet place.
It is a quiet folding,
like going to sleep in
the comfortable family home.
When everyone goes to sleep
the house folds up.
The windows shut their eyes.
If you are inside you are automatically folded.
If you are outside walking by the folded house
you feel so lonesome you think you are going crazy.

You are not going crazy.
You are beginning to fold up in your own single way.
You feel your edges move toward the center,
your heart like a folded blanket unfolding
and folding in with everything contained.
You feel you do not need anyone to love you any more
because you already feel everything,
you feel it, you fold it, and for a while now,
it will quietly rest.

Adios

It is a good word, rolling off the tongue
no matter what language you were born with.
Use it. Learn where it begins,
the small alphabet of departure,
how long it takes to think of it,
then say it, then be heard.

Marry it. More than any golden ring,
it shines, it shines.
Wear it on every finger
till your hands dance,
touching everything easily,
letting everything, easily, go.

Strap it to your back like wings.
Or a kite-tail. The stream of air behind a jet.
If you are known for anything,
let it be the way you rise out of sight
when your work is finished.

Think of things that linger: leaves,
cartons and napkins, the damp smell of mold.

Think of things that disappear.

Think of what you love best,
what brings tears into your eyes.

Something that said *adios* to you
before you knew what it meant
or how long it was for.

Explain little, the word explains itself.
Later perhaps. Lessons following lessons,
like silence following sound.

from

HUGGING THE JUKEBOX

(1982)

Lights from Other Windows

Driving west tonight, the city dissolves behind us.
I keep feeling we're going farther than we're going,
a journey that started in the deep inkwell
out of which all our days are written.
Nothing is said to indicate a monument,
yet I perch on the edge of some new light.
The hills could crack open and a pointed beam,
like the beams on miners' hats, could pick us off this road.
Signals blinking, we arrive in a bright room
of greetings and hands. But when the stories spill,
I feel myself floating off alone into that night we just left,
that cool black bag of darkness, where black deer
nibbled invisible grasses and black fences divided one thing
from the next. A voice in my earliest ears *not this, not this*
and the lit windows of childhood rise up,
the windows of houses where strangers lived,
light slanting across black roads,
that light which said *what a small flicker is given
to each of us to know*. For seconds I dreamed their rooms
and tables, was comforted by promise of a billion other lives.
Like stars. Like knowing the Milky Way
is made of more stars than any naked eye can count.
Like having someplace to go when your glowing restlessness
lifts you out of rooms, becomes a wing,
takes you farther than you will have traveled
when your own life ends.

Daily

These shriveled seeds we plant
corn kernel   dried bean
poke into loosened soil
cover over with measured fingertips

These T-shirts we fold into
perfect white squares

These tortillas we slice and fry to crisp strips
This rich egg scrambled in a gray clay bowl

This bed whose covers I straighten
smoothing edges till blue quilt fits brown blanket
and nothing hangs out

This envelope I address
so the name balances like a cloud
in the center of the sky

This page I type and retype
This table I dust till the scarred wood shines
This bundle of clothes I wash and hang and wash again
like flags we share, a country so close
no one needs to name it

The days are nouns: touch them
The hands are churches that worship the world

Making a Fist

For the first time, on the road north of Tampico,
I felt the life sliding out of me,
a drum in the desert, harder and harder to hear.
I was seven, I lay in the car
watching palm trees swirl a sickening pattern past the glass.
My stomach was a melon split wide inside my skin.

'How do you know if you are going to die?'
I begged my mother.
We had been traveling for days.
With strange confidence she answered,
'When you can no longer make a fist.'

Years later I smile to think of that journey,
the borders we must cross separately,
stamped with our unanswerable woes.
I who did not die, who am still living,
still lying in the backseat behind all my questions,
clenching and opening one small hand.

Famous

The river is famous to the fish.

The loud voice is famous to silence,
which knew it would inherit the earth
before anybody said so.

The cat sleeping on the fence is famous to the birds
watching him from the birdhouse.

The tear is famous, briefly, to the cheek.

The idea you carry close to your bosom
is famous to your bosom.

The boot is famous to the earth,
more famous than the dress shoe,
which is famous only to floors.

The bent photograph is famous to the one who carries it
and not at all famous to the one who is pictured.

I want to be famous to shuffling men
who smile while crossing streets,
sticky children in grocery lines,
famous as the one who smiled back.

I want to be famous in the way a pulley is famous,
or a buttonhole, not because it did anything spectacular,
but because it never forgot what it could do.

So Much Happiness

(for Michael)

It is difficult to know what to do with so much happiness.
With sadness there is something to rub against,
a wound to tend with lotion and cloth.
When the world falls in around you, you have pieces to pick up,
something to hold in your hands, like ticket stubs or change.

But happiness floats.
It doesn't need you to hold it down.
It doesn't need anything.
Happiness lands on the roof of the next house, singing,
and disappears when it wants to.
You are happy either way.
Even the fact that you once lived in a peaceful tree house
and now live over a quarry of noise and dust
cannot make you unhappy.
Everything has a life of its own,
it too could wake up filled with possibilities
of coffee cake and ripe peaches,
and love even the floor which needs to be swept,
the soiled linens and scratched records...

Since there is no place large enough
to contain so much happiness,
you shrug, you raise your hands, and it flows out of you
into everything you touch. You are not responsible.
You take no credit, as the night sky takes no credit
for the moon, but continues to hold it, and share it,
and in that way, be known.

Hugging the Jukebox

On an island the soft hue of memory,
moss green, kerosene yellow, drifting, mingling
in the Caribbean Sea,
a six-year-old named Alfred
learns all the words to all the songs
on his grandparents' jukebox, and sings them.
To learn the words is not so hard.
Many barmaids and teenagers have done as well.
But to sing as Alfred sings –
how can a giant whale live in the small pool of his chest?
How can there be breakers this high, notes crashing
at the beach of the throat,
and a reef of coral so enormous only the fishes know its size?

The grandparents watch. They can't sing.
They don't know who this voice is, trapped in their grandson's body.
The boy whose parents sent him back to the island
to chatter mango-talk and scrap with chickens –
three years ago he didn't know the word 'sad'
Now he strings a hundred passionate sentences on a single line.
He bangs his fist so they will raise the volume.

What will they do together in their old age?
It is hard enough keeping yourself alive.
And this wild boy, loving nothing but music –
he'll sing all night, hugging the jukebox.
When a record pauses, that live second before dropping down,
Alfred hugs tighter, arms stretched wide,
head pressed on the luminous belly. 'Now!' he yells.
A half-smile when the needle breathes again.

They've tried putting him to bed, but he sings in bed.
Even in Spanish – and he doesn't speak Spanish!
Sings and screams, wants to go back to the jukebox.
O mama I was born with a trumpet in my throat
    spent all these years tryin' to cough it up...

He can't even read yet. He can't *tell time*.
But he sings, and the chairs in this old dance hall jerk to attention.
The grandparents lean on the counter, shaking their heads.
The customers stop talking and stare, goosey bumps surfacing on
        their arms.
His voice carries out to the water where boats are tied
and sings for all of them, *a wave*.
For the hens, now roosting in trees,
for the mute boy next door, his second-best friend.
And for the hurricane, now brewing near Barbados –
a week forward neighbors will be hammering boards over their
        windows,
rounding up dogs and fishing lines,
the generators will quit with solemn clicks in every yard.

But Alfred, hugging a sleeping jukebox, the names of the tunes
        gone dark,
will still be singing, doubly loud now, teasing his grandmother,
'Put a coin in my mouth!' and believing what she wants to believe;
this is not the end of the island, or the tablets this life has been
scribbled on, or the song.

Utila, Honduras

from

YELLOW GLOVE

(1986)

Trying to Name What Doesn't Change

Roselva says the only thing that doesn't change
is train tracks. She's sure of it.
The train changes, or the weeds that grow up spidery
by the side, but not the tracks.
I've watched one for three years, she says,
and it doesn't curve, doesn't break, doesn't grow.

Peter isn't sure. He saw an abandoned track
near Sabinas, Mexico, and says a track without a train
is a changed track. The metal wasn't shiny any more.
The wood was split and some of the ties were gone.

Every Tuesday on Morales Street
butchers crack the necks of a hundred hens.
The widow in the tilted house
spices her soup with cinnamon.
Ask her what doesn't change.

Stars explode.
The rose curls up as if there is fire in the petals.
The cat who knew me is buried under the bush.

The train whistle still wails its ancient sound
but when it goes away, shrinking back
from the walls of the brain,
it takes something different with it every time.

The Use of Fiction

A boy claims he saw you on a bicycle last week,
touring his neighborhood. 'West Cypress Street!' he shouts,
as if your being there and his seeing you
were some sort of benediction.
To be alive, to be standing outside
on a tender February evening...
'It was a blue bicycle, ma'am, your braid was flying,
I said hello and you laughed, remember?'

You almost tell him your bicycle seat is thick with dust,
the tires have been flat for months.
But his face, that radiant flower, says you are his friend,
he has told his mother your name.
Maybe this is a clear marble
he will hide in his sock drawer for months.
So who now, in a universe of figures,
would deny West Cypress Street,
throwing up clouds into this literal sky?
'Yes, amigo' – hand on shoulder –
'It was I.'

Yellow Glove

What can a yellow glove mean in a world of motorcars and governments?

I was small, like everyone. Life was a string of precautions: Don't kiss the squirrel before you bury him, don't suck candy, pop balloons, drop watermelons, watch TV. When the new gloves appeared one Christmas, tucked in soft tissue, I heard it trailing me: Don't lose the yellow gloves.

I was small, there was too much to remember. One day, waving at a stream – the ice had cracked, winter chipping down, soon we would sail boats and roll into ditches – I let a glove go. Into the stream, sucked under the street. Since when did streets have mouths? I walked home on a desperate road. Gloves cost money. We didn't have much. I would tell no one. I would wear the yellow glove that was left and keep the other hand in a pocket. I knew my mother's eyes had tears they had not cried yet, I didn't want to be the one to make them flow. It was the prayer I spoke secretly, folding socks, lining up donkeys in windowsills. *To be good*, a promise made to the roaches who scouted my closet at night. *If you don't get in my bed, I will be good*. And they listened. I had a lot to fulfill.

The months rolled down like towels out of a machine. I sang and drew and fattened the cat. Don't scream, don't lie, don't cheat, don't fight – you could hear it anywhere. A pebble could show you how to be smooth, tell the truth. A field could show how to sleep without walls. A stream could remember how to drift and change – next June I was stirring the stream like a soup, telling my brother dinner would be ready if he'd only hurry up with the bread, when I saw it. The yellow glove draped on a twig. A muddy survivor. A quiet flag.

Where had it been in the three gone months? I could wash it, fold it in my winter drawer with its sister, no one in that world would ever know. There were miracles on Harvey Street. Children walked home in yellow light. Trees were reborn and gloves traveled far, but returned. A thousand miles later, what can a yellow glove mean in a world of bankbooks and stereos?

Part of the difference between floating and going down.

Two Countries

Skin remembers how long the years grow
when skin is not touched, a gray tunnel
of singleness, feather lost from the tail
of a bird, swirling onto a step,
swept away by someone who never saw
it was a feather. Skin ate, walked,
slept by itself, knew how to raise a
see-you-later hand. But skin felt
it was never seen, never known as
a land on the map, nose like a city,
hip like a city, gleaming dome of the mosque
and the hundred corridors of cinnamon and rope.

Skin had hope, that's what skin does.
Heals over the scarred place, makes a road.
Love means you breathe in two countries.
And skin remembers – silk, spiny grass,
deep in the pocket that is skin's secret own.
Even now, when skin is not alone,
it remembers being alone and thanks something larger
that there are travelers, that people go places
larger than themselves.

Pakistan with Open Arms

Tonight in Karachi, a man drapes
jasmine garlands over his wrist
and looks both ways.
It is the hour of the walk,
when men and women come slowly forth
from houses, kitchens,
their strides growing long and musical,
sky finally softening its grip.
Whatever they talked about in the day
stands back to let them pass.

In some languages, a voice asking
a question goes up at the end
and an answer slopes toward the sea.
Maybe now the turtles are stepping
from their nests at the beach,
the huge shrine of their eggs behind them.
Maybe the fabulous painted buses
are cooling their engines at the lot.

How could I have seen, twenty years ago,
a night when a string of fragrant flowers
would be all I desired?
In the peaked shadow of his house
a man reads a map on which deserts
and mountains are different colors.
Each province has its own woven rugs
and speckled red hats.
He wishes to walk in a hundred villages
where people he will never meet are walking.

Into my arms I gather the quiet avenue,
the patience of curbs.
A family relaxes on a sweep of public grass.
Their shirts are cotton and silk.

They visit quietly as the moon comes speaking
its simple round name.
I gather them into me, saying,
This is the thunderous city.
This is the person who once was afraid.

Rain

A teacher asked Paul
what he would remember
from third grade, and he sat
a long time before writing
'this year sumbody tutched me
on the sholder'
and turned his paper in.
Later she showed it to me
as an example of her wasted life.
The words he wrote were large
as houses in a landscape.
He wanted to go inside them
and live, he could fill in
the windows of 'o' and 'd'
and be safe while outside
birds building nests in drainpipes
knew nothing of the coming rain.

Catalogue Army

Something has happened to my name.
It now appears on catalogues
for towels and hiking equipment,
dresses spun in India,
hand-colored prints of parrots and eggs.
Fifty tulips are on their way
if I will open the door.
Dishrags from North Carolina
unstack themselves in the Smoky Mountains
and make a beeline for my sink.

I write a postcard to my cousin:
this is what it is like to live in America.
Individual tartlet pans congregate
in the kitchen, chiming my name.
Porcelain fruit boxes float above tables,
sterling silver ice cream cone holders
twirl upside down on the cat's dozing head.

For years I developed radar against malls.
So what is it that secretly applauds
this army of catalogues marching upon my house?
I could be in the bosom of poverty, still they arrive.
I could be dead, picked apart by vultures,
still they would tell me
what socks to wear in my climbing boots.

Stay true, catalogues, protect me
from the wasteland where whimsy and impulse
never camp.
Be my companion on this journey between dusts,
between vacancy and that smiling stare
that is citizen of every climate
but customer to nothing,
even air.

What He Said to His Enemies

He could hear them off in the forest,
massive branches breaking:
you are no good, will never be any good.

Sometimes they followed him,
rubbing out his tracks.
They wanted him to get lost
in the world of trees,
stand silently forever, holding up his hands.

At night he watched
the streetlamp's light
soaking into his lawn.
He could bathe in its cool voice,
roll over to a whole different view.
What made them think
the world's room was so small?

On the table he laid out his clothes,
arranging the cuffs.
What he said to his enemies
was a window pushed high as it would go.
Come in, look for me where you think
I am. Then when you see no one is there,
we can talk.

from

RED SUITCASE

(1994)

Travel Alarm

Because everything still bears
the sweet iron taste of experiment,
a penny pressed to the tongue,
the boy places his mother's
little clock in the broiler.
Way back, down deep,
so she won't see when
she bakes the muffins.

Once she says, What's that smell
in here? Like truck tires
at a car lot – and he grins,
by now having forgotten,
but liking strange odors
that rise in the midst of any day,
strange bells, even the maniac
who kept roaring around their block
till his mother called the police.

Each morning he begs his parents
not to read the newspaper, knowing
how their faces go half-blank
and mad, their hands turn
and turn never finding
the right page.

But the secret woman keeps pitching
the rolled paper into their yard,
the woman called Willie or Freddie,
whom he caught a glimpse of once,
pulling away in her long arrow
of a car.

Later he asks, is it still morning?
If it's noon, why is it so dark?
Some evening when his mother pulls
the broiler wide to find
her melted ring of hours,
now crisp as a wedding collar,
and the two frozen hands,
he'll feel far away,
as if he didn't do anything
leading up to it.

But when she likes the hard new shine
glossing the puckered 3 and
sunken 8, when she says
Now we can never be late

and laughs, and laughs,
the sound of a storm coming
that lifts the air in its path,

when she hands it back to him
and he winds the little key
to hear it ring! Still –
the wild buzz that woke them up
in a hundred different towns –
he'll feel how morning and evening
run together, how bad and good can melt
into something entirely else.

They'll tell his father
when he steps from the darkroom
blinking, they'll say
We have a surprise for you,
and hold it up. It will take him
a long moment even to know
what it was.

Standing together
on the edge of dinnertime
and night, the table half-set
but nothing missing,
no one wishing for any
impossible season,
– when I was smaller,
when you'll be older –
even the trees outside
that should be thinking autumn now
still lit by an endless minute
of green.

From Here to There

Everything needs readiness,
baskets emptied,
gladiolus spear placed in
a glass.

Before you begin,
before you let yourself move
from here to there,
you attend to little things,
a cat's mouth open and crying,
a thin parade of ants
along the sill.

Something in the way we are made
wants order. Wants three pillows
lined across the head of the bed,
wants porches swept and shades raised.

Before we begin. Before we head into
those secret rooms no one else
has cleaned for years,
where memories rest in heaps,
without cabinets,
and have only to be touched lightly
to shine.

The Attic and Its Nails

It's hard up there. You dig in a box for whatever the moment requires: sweater, wreath, the other half of the walkie-talkie, and find twelve things you forgot about which delay the original search, since now that you found them you have to think about them. Do I want to keep this, bring it downstairs? Of course your life feels very different from the life you had when you packed it up there. Maybe your life has another kind of room in it now, maybe it feels more crowded. Maybe you think looking at this old ceramic cup with the pocked white glaze that you made in college would uplift you in the mornings. Your search takes on an urgent ratlike quality as you rip paper out of boxes, shredding and piling it. Probably by now you've stood up too fast and speared your head on one of the nails that holds the roof shingles down. They're lined up all along the rafters, poking through, aimed. Now you have to think about tetanus, rusty nails, the hearty human skull. A little dizzy for awhile, you're too occupied to remember what sent you up into the dark.

Voices

I will never taste cantaloupe
without tasting the summers
you peeled for me and placed
face-up on my china breakfast plate.

You wore tightly laced shoes
and smelled like the roses in your yard.
I buried my face in your
soft petaled cheek.

How could I know you carried
a deep well of tears?
I thought grandmas were as calm
as their stoves.
How could I know your voice
had been pushed down hard inside you
like a plug?

You stood back in a crowd.
But your garden flourished and answered
your hands. Sometimes I think of the land
you loved, gone to seed now,
gone to someone else's name,
and I want to walk among silent women
scattering light. Like a debt I owe
my grandma. To lift whatever cloud it is
made them believe speaking is for others.
As once we removed treasures from your
sock drawer and held them one-by-one,
ocean shell, Chinese button, against the sky.

His Secret

The field wraps around him.
He takes in his fist the 3-winged grasses,
the stick shaped like a Y.

Filling his bag with fallen petals,
shiny wrappers, husks.

Filling his eyes.

He is welcoming the bent weed,
spinning the hay.

Tying the shoelace
to the stone.

No one answers his questions better
than the split brick he hit
with a hammer.

Above him, a hundred flying birds call out
'Alone! Alone! Alone!'

*

At the heart of the apple,
at the heart of the worm.

A boy filled a bottle with water.
He let it sit.
Three days later it held the power
of three days.

Violin

It's been sleeping under the bed
for twenty years.

Once I let it out every day.
Neighbors picked up bits of music
wedged into grass.

I stroked the resiny hairs of bow.
All my tutors, lunatics, but my mother
left us alone.

Sometimes a sonata
broke in the middle –
I stitched it together
slowly, slowly.

Graceful shoulders,
elegant neck –
what do you know now
that you didn't know then?

Living with Mistakes

They won't wear boots.
They march ahead of us
into our rooms, dripping.

Give them a chair.
Where they sit,
the fabric will be wet
for days.
We have to talk about
everything else
in their presence.

Valentine for Ernest Mann

You can't order a poem like you order a taco.
Walk up to the counter, say, 'I'll take two'
and expect it to be handed back to you
on a shiny plate.

Still, I like your spirit.
Anyone who says, 'Here's my address,
write me a poem,' deserves something in reply.
So I'll tell a secret instead:
poems hide. In the bottoms of our shoes,
they are sleeping. They are the shadows
drifting across our ceilings the moment
before we wake up. What we have to do
is live in a way that lets us find them.

Once I knew a man who gave his wife
two skunks for a valentine.
He couldn't understand why she was crying.
'I thought they had such beautiful eyes.'
And he was serious. He was a serious man
who lived in a serious way. Nothing was ugly
just because the world said so. He really
liked those skunks. So, he re-invented them
as valentines and they became beautiful.
At least, to him. And the poems that had been hiding
in the eyes of skunks for centuries
crawled out and curled up at his feet.

Maybe if we re-invent whatever our lives give us
we find poems. Check your garage, the odd sock
in your drawer, the person you almost like, but not quite.
And let me know.

What Brings Us Out

Something about pumpkins caused
the man who had not spoken in three years
to lean forward, cough, open his mouth.
How the room heaved into silence,
his words enormous in that air:
'I won't...be...afraid...
of my...father...anymore.'
And what silence followed,
as if each heart had spoken
its most secret terror,
had combed the tangled clump
for the hardest line
and pulled it, intact,
from the mass.

I bless that man forever
for his courage, his voice
which started with one thing
and went to many, opening up and up
to the rim of the world.
So much silence had given him
a wisdom which held us all at bay,
amazed. Sometimes when I see
mountains of pumpkins by the roadside,
or watermelons, a hill of autumn gourds
piled lavishly on crates, I think
perhaps this one, or that, were it to
strike someone right,
this curl of hardened stalk,
this pleated skin...

or, on an old bureau drawer,
the vegetable-like roundness of a glass knob
that the baby turns and turns
emerging, later, from a complicated dream...

the huge navigational face of a radio
which never worked while I was alive
but gave me more to go on than most sounds:
how what brings us out may be
small as that black arrow, swinging
the wide arc, the numbers where silent voices lived,
how fast you had to turn to make it move.

Saved

Once I burned a man's letters
in a metal can in front of him

a wisp of that smoke returns
in the clear breath of mountains
his rueful look the flare of anger
that struck the match

nothing we'd planned to happen did
we have all been saved so many times

why I should think of this
years later in such elegant air
not wondering what happened to him
or feeling regret but thinking instead
how the signs on abandoned motels
west of Langtry Texas have faded more
each year

EXCELLENT BEDS
just a pale red whisper now
TILE BATHROOMS
ghost of a promise
receding into stucco wall
SLEEP WELL HERE

Shoulders

A man crosses the street in rain,
stepping gently, looking two times north and south:
because his son is asleep on his shoulder.

No car must splash him.
No car drive too near to his shadow.

This man carries the world's most sensitive cargo
but he's not marked.
Nowhere does his jacket say FRAGILE,
HANDLE WITH CARE.

His ear fills up with breathing.
He hears the hum of a boy's dream
deep inside him.

We're not going to be able
to live in this world
if we're not willing to do what he's doing
with one another.

The road will only be wide.
The rain will never stop falling.

from

FUEL

(1998)

Muchas Gracias por Todo

This plane has landed thanks to God and his mercy.
That's what they say in Jordan when the plane sets down.

What do they say in our country? Don't stand up till we tell
you.
Stay in your seats. Things may have shifted.

This river has not disappeared thanks to that one big storm
when the water was almost finished.

We used to say thanks to the springs
but the springs dried up so we changed it.

This rumor tells no truth thanks to people.
This river walk used to be better when no one came.

What about the grapes? Thanks to the grapes
we have more than one story to tell.

Thanks to a soft place in the middle of the evening.
Thanks to three secret hours before dawn.

These deer are seldom seen because of their shyness.
If you see one you count yourselves among the lucky on the
earth.

Your eyes get quieter.
These deer have nothing to say to us.

Thanks to the fan, we are still breathing.
Thanks to the small toad that lives in cool mud at the base of
        the zinnias.

Bill's Beans
(for William Stafford)

Under the leaves, they're long and curling.
I pull a perfect question-mark and two lean twins,
feeling the magnetic snap of stem, the ripened weight.
At the end of a day, the earth smells thirsty.
He left his brown hat, his shovel, and his pen.
I don't know how deep bean roots go.
We could experiment.
He left the sky over Oregon and the fluent trees.
He gave us our lives that were hiding under our feet,
saying, You know what to do.
So we'll take these beans
back into the house and steam them.
We'll eat them one by one with our fingers,
the clean click and freshness.
We'll thank him forever for our breath,
and the brevity of bean.

Wedding Cake

Once on a plane
a woman asked me to hold her baby
and disappeared.
I figured it was safe,
our being on a plane and all.
How far could she go?

She returned one hour later,
having changed her clothes
and washed her hair.
I didn't recognise her.

By this time the baby
and I had examined
each other's necks.
We had cried a little.
I had a silver bracelet
and a watch.
Gold studs glittered
in the baby's ears.
She wore a tiny white dress
leafed with layers
like a wedding cake.

I did not want
to give her back.

The baby's curls coiled tightly
against her scalp,
another alphabet.
I read *new new new.*
My mother gets tired.
I'll chew your hand.

The baby left my skirt crumpled,
my lap aching.
Now I'm her secret guardian,
the little nub of dream
that rises slightly
but won't come clear.

As she grows,
as she feels ill at ease,
I'll bob my knee.

What will she forget?
Whom will she marry?
He'd better check with me.
I'll say once she flew
dressed like a cake
between two doilies of cloud.
She could slip the card into a pocket,
pull it out.
Already she knew the small finger
was funnier than the whole arm.

Because of Libraries We Can Say These Things

She is holding the book close to her body,
carrying it home on the cracked sidewalk,
down the tangled hill.
If a dog runs at her again, she will use the book as a shield.

She looked hard among the long lines
of books to find this one.
When they start talking about money,
when the day contains such long and hot places,
she will go inside.
An orange bed is waiting.
Story without corners.
She will have two families.
They will eat at different hours.

She is carrying a book past the fire station
and the five-and-dime.
What this town has not given her
the book will provide; a sheep,
a wilderness of new solutions.
The book has already lived through its troubles.
The book has a calm cover, a straight spine.

When the step returns to itself
as the best place for sitting,
and the old men up and down the street
are latching their clippers,

she will not be alone.
She will have a book to open
and open and open.
Her life starts here.

Elevator

We jumped in, trusting
the slow swish of heavy doors,

punching 7, 9, 12.
O swoon of rising stomach! Then a sudden drop.

We took turns popping envelopes into the mail chute
& watching them whiz by from a lower floor.

Where are you? Calling down the tunnel,
sweet high ding, nobody's dinnerbell.

In stepped the lady with a fur muff,
her elegant gentleman smelling of New York.

We sobered our faces, bit the glinting arrows
while our father sorted receipts off the lobby.

Goodbye! we called to him again & again.
His desk wore a little spike.

Where are you going?
We are going!

Breathing rich perfume & dust
ground into burgundy carpet,

we glistened in the polished edge
of everything that didn't belong to us,

suitcases, humming radios,
brass locks, canisters for ash.

With nowhere to go we became
specialists in Ups & Downs.

Brother! I cried, as he rose to the penthouse without me.
Sister! He wailed, as I sank deep into the ground.

Eye Test

The D is desperate.
The B wants to take a vacation,
live on a billboard, be broad and brave.
The E is mad at the R for upstaging him.
The little c wants to be a big C if possible,
and the P pauses long between thoughts.

How much better to be a story, story.
Can you read me?

We have to live on this white board
together like a neighborhood.
We would rather be the tail of a cloud,
one letter becoming another,
or lost in a boy's pocket
shapeless as lint,
the same boy who squints to read us
believing we convey a secret message.
   Be his friend.
We are so tired of meaning nothing.

One Boy Told Me

Music lives inside my legs.
It's coming out when I talk.

I'm going to send my valentines
to people you don't even know.

Oatmeal cookies make my throat gallop.
Grown-ups keep their feet on the ground

when they swing. I hate that.
Look at those 2 o's with a smash in the middle –

that spells goodbye.
Don't ever say 'purpose' again,
let's throw the word out.

Don't talk big to me.
I'm carrying my box of faces.
If I want to change faces I will.

Yesterday faded
but tomorrow's in BOLDFACE.

When I grow up my old names
will live in the house
where we live now.
I'll come and visit them.

Only one of my eyes is tired.
The other eye and my body aren't.

Is it true all metal was liquid first?
Does that mean if we bought our car earlier
they could have served it
in a cup?

There's a stopper in my arm
that's not going to let me grow any bigger.
I'll be like this always, small.

And I will be deep water too.
Wait. Just wait. How deep is the river?
Would it cover the tallest man with his hands in the air?

Your head is a souvenir.

When you were in New York I could see you
in real life walking in my mind.

I'll invite a bee to live in your shoe.
What if you found your shoe
full of honey?

What if the clock said 6:92
instead of 6:30? Would you be scared?

My tongue is the car wash
for the spoon.

Can noodles swim?

My toes are dictionaries.
Do you need any words?

From now on I'll only drink white milk
on January 26.

What does minus mean?
I never want to minus you.

Just think – no one has ever seen
inside this peanut before!

It is hard being a person.

I do and don't love you —
isn't that happiness?

Boy and Mom at the Nutcracker Ballet

There's no talking in this movie.

> It's not a movie! Just watch the dancers.
> They tell the story through their dancing

Why is the nutcracker mean?

> I think because the little boy broke him.

Did the little boy mean to?

> Probably not.

Why did the nutcracker stab his sword through the mouse king?
I liked the mouse king.

> So did I. I don't know. I wish that part wasn't in it.

You can see that girl's underpants.

> No, not underpants. It's a costume called a 'tutu'.

That's the same word as 'grandma' in Hawaiian!
Are those really gems on their costumes?
Do they get to keep them?
Is that really snow coming down?

> No, it can't be, it would melt and their feet get wet.

I think it's white paper.

> Aren't they beautiful?

They are very beautiful. But what do the dancers do
when we can't see them, when they're off the stage
and they're not dancing?
Do you have any more pistachios in your purse?

Always Bring a Pencil

There will not be a test.
It does not have to be
a Number 2 pencil.

But there will be certain things –
the quiet flush of waves,
ripe scent of fish,
smooth ripple of the wind's second name –
that prefer to be written about
in pencil.

It gives them more room
to move around.

Glint

My grandmother mentioned only once how the piano teacher she had as a girl leaned over her too closely at the keys. His damp lips grazed her cheek or maybe they touched her mouth for a minute. My grandmother never felt comfortable with the piano after that. I think a little more music could have helped her life. I played her piano sometimes. Dust rose in little clouds from the cracks between the keys. A few keys had lost their voices. My grandmother told me some things but not enough. We had a sweetness between us. What happened to the piano teacher? His lips parting ever so slightly over middle C, eyes pinned to the ripe notes on the sheet...could he help it what they reminded him of? Here I am trying to gather her lost kisses from the air. They're drifting just outside the tune.

Alphabet

One by one
the old people
of our neighborhood
are going up
into the air

their yards
still wear
small white narcissus
sweetening winter

their stones
glisten
under the sun
but one by one
we are losing
their housecoats
their formal phrasings
their cupcakes

When I string their names
on the long cord

when I think how
there is almost no one left
who remembers
what stood in that
brushy spot
ninety years ago

when I pass their yards
and the bare peach tree
bends a little

when I see their rusted chairs
sitting in the same spots

what will be forgotten
falls over me
like the sky
over our whole neighborhood

or the time my plane
circled high above our street
the roof of our house
dotting the tiniest
'i'

Hidden

If you place a fern
under a stone
the next day it will be
nearly invisible
as if the stone has
swallowed it.

If you tuck the name of a loved one
under your tongue too long
without speaking it
it becomes blood
sigh
the little sucked-in breath of air
hiding everywhere
beneath your words.

No one sees
the fuel that feeds you.

Lost

notices   flutter

　　from   telephone   poles

　　　until   they   fade

OUR SWEET TABBY   AFRAID OF EVERYTHING

BIG GRAY CAT   HE IS OUR ONLY CHILD

SIBERIAN HUSKY   NEEDS HIS MEDICINE

FEMALE SCHNAUZER   WE ARE SICK WITH WORRY

　　　all night I imagine their feet
　　　tapping up the sidewalk
　　under the blooming crepe myrtle
　　　and the swoon of jasmine
　　　　into the secret hedges
　　　　　　into the dark cool caves
　　　　of the banana-palm grove
　　　and we cannot catch them
　　　or know what they are thinking
　　when they go so far from home

OUR BELOVED TURTLE   RED DOT ON FOREHEAD
VEGETARIAN   NAME OF KALI

please   please   please

　　if you see them

call me   call me   call me

Books We Haven't Touched in Years

The person who wrote YES!
in margins
disappeared.

Someone else
tempers her enthusiasms,
makes a small 'v'
on its side
for lines
worth returning to.

A farmer
stares deeply
at a winter field,
envisioning
rich rows of corn.

In the mild tone
of farmers, says
Well, good luck.

What happens to us?

He doesn't dance
beside the road.

The Rider

A boy told me
if he roller-skated fast enough
his loneliness couldn't catch up to him,

the best reason I ever heard
for trying to be a champion.

What I wonder tonight
pedaling hard down King William Street
is if it translates to bicycles.

A victory! To leave your loneliness
panting behind you on some street corner
while you float free into a cloud of sudden azaleas,
pink petals that have never felt loneliness,
no matter how slowly they fell.

Fuel

Even at this late date, sometimes I have to look up
the word 'receive'. I received his deep
and interested gaze.

A bean plant flourishes under the rain of sweet words.
Tell what you think – I'm listening.

The story ruffled its twenty leaves.

*

Once my teacher set me on a high stool
for laughing. She thought the eyes
of my classmates would whittle me to size,
But they said otherwise.

We'd laugh too if we knew how.

I pinned my gaze out the window
on a ripe line of sky.

That's where I was going.

Across the Bay

If we throw our eyes way out to sea,
they thank us. All those corners
we've made them sit down in lately,
those objects with dust along
their seams.

Out here eyes find the edge
that isn't one.
Gray water, streak of pink,
little tap of sun,
and that storm off to the right
that seems to like us now.

How far can the wind carry
whatever lets go? Light
shining from dead stars
cradles our sleep. Secret light
no one reads by –
who owns that beam?
Who follows it far enough?

The month our son turned five
we drove between cotton fields
down to the bay. Thick layers
of cloud pouring into one another
as tractors furrowed the earth,
streams of gulls dipping down
behind. We talked about
the worms in their beaks.
How each thing on earth
searches out what it needs,
if it's lucky. And always
another question – *what if?*
what if?

Some day you'll go so far away
I'll die for missing you,
like millions of mothers
before me – how many friends
I suddenly have! Across the bay
a ship will be passing, tiny dot
between two ports meaning nothing
to me, carrying cargo useless to my life
but I'll place my eyes on it
as if it held me up. Or you rode
that boat.

Boy and Egg

Every few minutes, he wants
to march the trail of flattened rye grass
back to the house of muttering
hens. He too could make
a bed in hay. Yesterday the egg so fresh
it felt hot in his hand and he pressed it
to his ear while the other children
laughed and ran with a ball, leaving him,
so little yet, too forgetful in games,
ready to cry if the ball brushed him,
riveted to the secret of birds
caught up inside his fist,
not ready to give it over
to the refrigerator
or the rest of the day.

How Far Is It to the Land We Left?

On the first day of his life
the baby opens his eyes
and gets tired doing even that.
He cries when they place a cap on his head.
Too much, too much!

Later the whole world will touch him
and he won't even flinch.

Pause

The boy needed
to stop by the road.
What pleasure to let
the engine quit droning
inside the long heat,
to feel where they were.
Sometimes
she was struck by this
as if a plank had slapped
the back of her head.

They were thirsty
as grasses
leaning sideways
in the ditch,
Big Bluestem
and Little Barley,
Texas Cupgrass,
Hairy Crabgrass,
Green Sprangletop.
She could stop at a store
selling only grass names
and be happy.

They would pause
and the pause
seep into them,
fence post,
twisted wire,
brick chimney
without its house,
pollen taking flight
toward the cities.

Something would gather
back into place.
Take the word 'home'
for example,
often considered
to have an address.
How it could sweep across you
miles beyond the last
neat packages of ice
and nothing be wider
than its pulse.
Out here,
everywhere,
the boy looking away from her
across the fields.

Sad Mail

It's strange to think how letters used to be letters, letting you know someone liked you, saying pleasant dull things like, *How are you, we are fine*, making you wish for more but not weighing you, really. Now the letters are funnels of want, requests for favors, Please do what you can, Help me get into Yaddo (where I have never been), Tell my teachers I am a good student, Don't you think I would be excellent in that program overseas? I want to send everyone overseas. I want to be there myself, where my mail can't find me. It's startling to miss the sweet dim-witted reports of summers & boyfriends, journeys & pets, the scented lilac envelopes. Now the envelopes are long & white, letters begin *How long it has been since we really connected* & pole-vault into the request by the second paragraph. And no one ever says you have months to do this in. You have till tomorrow. I am lonely with my mail. Yesterday I went out walking before the mailman came, & the street was filled with carcasses of empty envelopes, dampened & tattered, the wings of exotic insects lost without their bodies. I wanted to bend & reclaim them, smooth them, fill them with unsigned notes, & drop them into my neighbor's shining boxes. One at a time.

Open House

I work as hard as I can
to have nothing to do.

Birds climb their rich ladder
of choruses.

They have tasted the top of the tree,
but they are not staying.

The whole sky says,
Your move.

Vocabulary of Dearness

How a single word
may shimmer and rise
off the page, a wafer of
syllabic light, a bulb
of glowing meaning,
whatever the word,
try 'tempestuous' or 'suffer',
any word you have held
or traded so it lives a new life
the size of two worlds.
Say you carried it
up a hill and it helped you
move. Without this
the days would be thin sticks
thrown down in a clutter of leaves,
and where is the rake?

Pollen

When weeds eat the playhouse
what does that say about the family?

The ball left at the base of the tree
loses its breath shrinking into

a stump or clump of dirt and the mole comes
and the earth drums up into little mounds

nobody kicks. Then what year is it?
Maybe the door to the big house opens and a man comes out.

A woman comes out drying her hands.
Dinner is almost ready but there's no one else

to eat it. Besides the man and the woman.
Maybe only the woman.

Or there's no dinner.
The door to the playhouse stuck open not swinging

and light comes through
replete with pollen of cedar and foxglove

and something else is going to be planted
in the ditch by the road

on the bank of the river but there will not be
a child to tell its story. How will that change the story?

If the fox puts on her lavender gloves just as you shut your eyes.
If in the night something touches your sleeping cheek

and startles you and it is the fox
but you forget to offer her tea in the playhouse

then what year would you be sipping?
What would that say about the person you became?

from

19 VARIETIES OF GAZELLE

(2002)

Flinn, on the Bus

Three hours after the buildings fell,
he took a seat beside me.
Fresh out of prison, after 24 months,
You're my first hello!
Going home to Mom,
a life he would make better this time,
how many times
he'd been swept along before,
to things he should never have...
drink and dope,
but now he'd take responsibility.
Lawyers had done him wrong
and women too. He thought
about revenge, now he was out.
But I'm in charge. I'll think
before I act. I don't ever
want to go there again.
Two wrongs don't make a right.
Somehow, in his mouth, that day,
it sounded new.
The light came through the window
on a gentle-eyed man in a
'Focus on the Game' T-shirt,
who had given up
assault with deadly weapons,
no more, no good!

A man who had not seen TV in weeks,
secluding in his cell so colleagues
wouldn't trip him up,
extend his stay.
Who had not heard the news.
We rolled through green Oklahoma,
the bus windows made all the trees look bent.

A trick of refraction –
Flinn looked at his free hands
more than the fields,
turned them over in his lap,
no snap judgments, no quick angers,
I'll stand back, look at what happens,
think calmly what my next step should be.
It was not hard to nod,
to wish him well. But could I tell
what had happened in the world
on his long-awaited day,
what twists of rage greater
than we could ever guess
had savaged skylines, thousands of lives?
I could not. He'd find out
soon enough. Flinn, take it easy.
Peace is rough.

September 11, 2001

Different Ways to Pray

There was the method of kneeling,
a fine method, if you lived in a country
where stones were smooth.
Women dreamed wistfully of
hidden corners where knee fit rock.
Their prayers, weathered rib bones,
small calcium words uttered in sequence,
as if this shedding of syllables could
fuse them to the sky.

There were men who had been shepherds so long
they walked like sheep.
Under the olive trees, they raised their arms –
Hear us! We have pain on earth!
We have so much pain there is no place to store it!
But the olives bobbed peacefully
in fragrant buckets of vinegar and thyme.
At night the men ate heartily, flat bread and white cheese,
and were happy in spite of the pain,
because there was also happiness.

Some prized the pilgrimage,
wrapping themselves in new white linen
to ride buses across miles of sand.
When they arrived at Mecca
they would circle the holy places,
on foot, many times,
they would bend to kiss the earth
and return, their lean faces housing mystery.

While for certain cousins and grandmother
the pilgrimage occurred daily,
lugging water from the spring
or balancing baskets of grapes.

These were the ones present at births,
humming quietly to perspiring mothers.
The ones stitching intricate needlework into children's dresses,
forgetting how easily children soil clothes.

There were those who didn't care about praying.
The young ones. The ones who had been to America,
They told the old ones, *you are wasting your time.*
   Time? The old ones prayed for the young ones.
They prayed for Allah to mend their brains,
for the twig, the round moon,
to speak suddenly in a commanding tone.

And occasionally there would be one
who did none of this,
the old man Fowzi, for example,
who beat everyone at dominoes,
insisted he spoke with God as he spoke with goats,
and was famous for his laugh.

My Father and the Figtree

For other fruits my father was indifferent.
He'd point at the cherry trees and say,
'See those? I wish they were figs.'
In the evenings he sat by our beds
weaving folktales like vivid little scarves.
They always involved a figtree.
Even when it didn't fit, he'd stick it in.
Once Joha was walking down the road
and he saw a figtree.
Or, he tied his donkey to a figtree and went to sleep.
Or, later when they caught and arrested him,
his pockets were full of figs.

At age six I ate a dried fig and shrugged.
'That's not what I'm talking about!' he said,
'I'm talking about a fig straight from the earth –
gift of Allah! – on a branch so heavy
it touches the ground.
I'm talking about picking the largest, fattest, sweetest fig
in the world and putting it in my mouth.'
(Here he'd stop and close his eyes.)

Years passed, we lived in many houses,
none had figtrees.
We had lima beans, zucchini, parsley, beets.
'Plant one!' my mother said,
but my father never did.
He tended garden half-heartedly, forgot to water,
let the okra get too big.
'What a dreamer he is. Look how many
things he starts and doesn't finish.'

The last time he moved, I had a phone call,
my father, in Arabic, chanting a song
I'd never heard. 'What's that?'

He took me out to the new yard.
There, in the middle of Dallas, Texas,
a tree with the largest, fattest,
sweetest figs in the world.
'It's a figtree song!' he said,
plucking his fruits like ripe tokens,
emblems, assurance
of a world that was always his own.

What Kind of Fool Am I?

He sang with abandon,
combing his black, black hair.
Each morning in the shower,
first in Arabic, rivery ripples
of song carrying him back
to his first beloved land,
then in English, where his repertoire
was short. *No kind at all!* we'd shout,
throwing ourselves into the brisk arc
of his cologne for a morning kiss.
But he gave us freedom to be fools
if we needed to, which we certainly
would later, which we all do now and then,
perhaps a father's greatest gift –
that blessing.

The Words Under the Words

(for Sitti Khadra, north of Jerusalem)

My grandmother's hands recognise grapes,
the damp shine of a goat's new skin.
When I was sick they followed me,
I woke from the long fever to find them
covering my head like cool prayers.

My grandmother's days are made of bread,
a round pat-pat and the slow baking.
She waits by the oven watching a strange car
circle the streets. Maybe it holds her son,
lost to America. More often, tourists,
who kneel and weep at mysterious shrines.
She knows how often mail arrives,
how rarely there is a letter.
When one comes, she announces it, a miracle,
listening to it read again and again
in the dim evening light.

My grandmother's voice says
nothing can surprise her.
Take her the shotgun wound and the crippled baby.
She knows the spaces we travel through,
the messages we cannot send – our voices are short
and would get lost on the journey.
Farewell to the husband's coat,
the ones she has loved and nourished,
who fly from her like seeds into a deep sky.
They will plant themselves. We will all die.

My grandmother's eyes say Allah is everywhere, even in death.
When she speaks of the orchard
and the new olive press,
when she tells the stories of Joha
and his foolish wisdoms,
He is her first thought, what she really thinks of is His name.

'Answer, if you hear the words under the words –
otherwise it is just a world
with a lot of rough edges,
difficult to get through, and our pockets
full of stones.'

The Man Who Makes Brooms

So you come with these maps in your head
and I come with voices chiding me to
'speak for my people'
and we march around like guardians of memory
till we find the man on the short stool
who makes brooms.

Thumb over thumb, straw over straw,
he will not look at us.
In his stony corner there is barely room
for baskets and thread,
much less the weight of our faces
staring at him from the street.
What he has lost or not lost is his secret.

You say he is like all the men,
the man who sells pistachios,
the man who rolls the rugs.
Older now, you find holiness in anything
that continues, dream after dream.
I say he is like nobody,
the pink seam he weaves
across the flat golden face of this broom
is its own shrine, and forget about the tears.

In the village the uncles will raise their *kefiyahs*
from dominoes to say, no brooms in America?
And the girls who stoop to sweep the courtyard
will stop for a moment and cock their heads.
It is a little song, this thumb over thumb,
but sometimes when you wait years
for the air to break open
and sense to fall out,
it may be the only one.

Jerusalem

Lunch in Nablus City Park

When you lunch in a town
which has recently known war
under a calm slate sky mirroring none of it,
certain words feel impossible in the mouth.
Casualty: too casual, it must be changed.
A short man stacks mounds of pita bread
on each end of the table, muttering
something about more to come.
Plump birds landing on park benches
surely had their eyes closed recently,
must have seen nothing of weapons or blockades.
When the woman across from you whispers
I don't think we can take it any more
and you say there are people praying for her
in the mountains of Himalaya and she says
Lady, it is not enough, then what?

A plate of *hummus*, dish of tomato,
friends dipping bread –
I will not marry till there is true love, says one,
throwing back her cascade of perfumed hair.
He says the University of Texas seems remote to him
as Mars, and last month he stayed in his house
for 26 days. He will not leave, he refuses to leave.
In the market they are selling
men's shoes with air vents, a beggar displays
the giant scab of leg he must drag
    from alley to alley,
and students argue about
the best ways to protest.

In summers, this café is full.
Today only our table sends laughter into the tree
What cannot be answered checkers the tablecloth
between the squares of white and red.

Where do the souls of hills hide
when there is shooting in the valleys?
What makes a man with a gun seem bigger
than a man with almonds? How can there be war
and the next day eating, a man stacking plates
on the curl of his arm, a table of people
toasting one another in languages of grace:
For you who came so far;
For you who held out, wearing a black scarf
to signify grief;
For you who believe true love can find you
amidst this atlas of tears linking one town
to its own memory of mortar,
when it was still a dream to be built
and people moved here, believing,
and someone with sky and birds in his heart
said this would be a good place for a park.

Red Brocade

The Arabs used to say,
When a stranger appears at your door,
feed him for three days
before asking who he is,
where he's come from,
where he's headed.
That way, he'll have strength
enough to answer.
Or, by then you'll be
such good friends
you don't care.

Let's go back to that.
Rice? Pine nuts?
Here, take the red brocade pillow.
My child will serve water
to your horse.

No, I was not busy when you came.
I was not preparing to be busy.
That's the armor everyone put on
to pretend they had a purpose
in the world.

I refuse to be claimed.
Your plate is waiting.
We will snip fresh mint
into your tea.

For the 500th Dead Palestinian, Ibtisam Bozieh

Little Sister Ibtisam,
our sleep flounders, our sleep tugs
the cord of your name.
Dead at 13, for staring through
the window into a gun barrel
which did not know you wanted to be
a doctor.

I would smooth your life in my hands,
pull you back. Had I stayed in your land,
I might have been dead too,
for something simple like staring
or shouting what was true
and getting kicked out of school.
I wandered stony afternoons
owning all their vastness.

Now I would give them to you,
guiltily, you, not me.
Throwing this ragged grief into the street,
scissoring news stories free from the page
but they live on my desk with letters, not cries.

How do we carry the endless surprise
of all our deaths? Becoming doctors
for one another, Arab, Jew,
instead of guarding tumors of pain
as if they hold us upright?

People in other countries speak easily
of being early, late.
Some will live to be eighty.
Some who never saw it
will not forget your face.

Those Whom We Do Not Know

*To feel the love of people whom we love is a fire
that feeds our life. But to feel the affection that
comes from those whom we do not know...
is something still greater and more beautiful...*

PABLO NERUDA

1

Because our country has entered
into war, we can have
no pleasant pauses any more –

instead, the nervous turning
one side to another,
each corner crowded by the far
but utterly particular
voices of the dead,

trees, fish, children,
calling, calling,
wearing the colorful plastic shoes
so beloved in the Middle East,
bleeding from the skull,
the sweet hollow along the neck.

I forget why. It's been changed.
For whatever it was
we will crush the vendor
who stacked sesame rings
on a tray
inside the steady gaze
of stones.
He will lose his balance
after years of perfect balance.

Catch him! Inside every sleep
he keeps falling.

2

I support all people on earth
who have bodies like and unlike my body,
skins and moles and old scars,
secret and public hair,
crooked toes. I support
those who have done nothing large,
sifter of lentils, sifter of wisdoms,
speak. If we have killed no one
in the name of anything bad or good,
may light feed our leafiest veins.

I support clothes in the wash-kettle,
a woman stirring and stirring
with stick, paddle, soaking out grime,
simple clothes the size of bodies
pinned to the sky.

3

What we learned left us.
None of it held.

Now the words ignite.
Slogans knot around necks
till faces bulge.

Windows of sand, doorways,
sense of shifting
each time you blink –

that dune? Used to be
a house. And the desert
soaking up echoes –

those whom we did not know
think they know us now.

Visit

Welcome to Abu Dhabi,
the Minister of Culture said.
You may hold my falcon as we visit.
He slipped a leather band around my arm
and urged the bird to step on board.
It wore a shapely leather hood.
Or otherwise, the host described,
the bird might pluck your very eyes.
My very eyes were blinking hard
behind the glasses that they wore.
The falcon's claws, so hooked and huge,
gripped firmly on the leather band.
I had to hold my arm out high.
My hand went numb. The heavens shone
a giant gold beyond our room.
1 had no memory why I'd come
to see this man.
A falcon dives, and rips, and kills!
I think he likes you though.
It was the most I could have hoped for then.
We mentioned art.
We drank some tea.
He offered to remove the hood.
I said the bird looked very good just wearing it.
All right by me.

The Small Vases from Hebron

Tip their mouths open to the sky.
Turquoise, amber,
the deep green with fluted handle,
pitcher the size of two thumbs,
tiny lip and graceful waist.

Here we place the smallest flower
which could have lived invisibly
in loose soil beside the road,
sprig of succulent rosemary,
bowing mint.

They grow deeper in the center of the table.

Here we entrust the small life,
thread, fragment, breath.
And it bends. It waits all day.
As the bread cools and the children
open their gray copybooks
to shape the letter that looks like
a chimney rising out of a house.

And what do the headlines say?

Nothing of the smaller petal
perfectly arranged inside the larger petal
or the way tinted glass filters light.
Men and boys, praying when they died,
fall out of their skins.
The whole alphabet of living,
heads and tails of words,
sentences, the way they said,
'Ya'Allah!' when astonished,
or 'ya'ani' for 'I mean' –

a crushed glass under the feet
still shines.
But the child of Hebron sleeps
with the thud of her brothers falling
and the long sorrow of the color red.

My Grandmother in the Stars

It is possible we will not meet again
on earth. To think this fills my throat
with dust. Then there is only the sky
tying the universe together.

Just now the neighbor's horse must be standing
patiently, hoof on stone, waiting for his day
to open. What you think of him,
and the village's one heroic cow,
is the knowledge I wish to gather.
I bow to your rugged feet,
the moth-eaten scarves that knot your hair.

Where we live in the world
is never one place. Our hearts,
those dogged mirrors, keep flashing us
moons before we are ready for them.
You and I on a roof at sunset,
our two languages adrift,
heart saying, Take this home with you,
never again,
and only memory making us rich.

19 Varieties of Gazelle

A gash of movement,
a spring of flight.

She saw them then
she did not see them.

The elegance of the gazelle
caught in her breath.

The next thing could have been weeping.

Rustic brown, a subtle spotted hue.

For years the Arab poets used 'gazelle'
to signify grace,
but when faced with a meadow of leaping gazelle
there were no words.

Does one gazelle prefer another
of her kind?

They soared like history
above an empty page.

Nearby, giant tortoises
were kissing.

What else had we seen in our lives?
Nothing better than 19 varieties of gazelle
running free at the wildlife sanctuary...

'Don't bother to go there,'
said a man at our hotel.
'It's too far.'

But we were on a small sandy island,
nothing was far!

We had hiked among stony ruins
to the Tree of Life.
We had photographed a sign that said
KEEP TO THE PATH in English and Arabic.

Where is the path?
Please tell me.
Does a gazelle have a path?
Is the whole air the path of the gazelle?

The sun was a hot hand on our heads.

Human beings have voices –
what have they done for us?

There is no gazelle
in today's headline.

The next thing could have been weeping...
Since when is a gazelle
wiser than people?

Gentle gazelle
dipping her head
into a pool of silver grass.

Bahrain

Jerusalem

Let's be the same wound if we must bleed.
Let's fight side by side, even if the enemy
is ourselves: I am yours, you are mine.
TOMMY OLOFSSON

I'm not interested in
who suffered the most.
I'm interested in
people getting over it.

Once when my father was a boy
a stone hit him on the head.
Hair would never grow there.
Our fingers found the tender spot
and its riddle: the boy who has fallen
stands up. A bucket of pears
in his mother's doorway welcomes him home.
The pears are not crying.
Later his friend who threw the stone
says he was aiming at a bird.
And my father starts growing wings.

Each carries a tender spot:
something our lives forgot to give us.
A man builds a house and says,
'I am native now.'
A woman speaks to a tree in place
of her son. And olives come.
A child's poem says,
'I don't like wars,
they end up with monuments.'
Hes painting a bird with wings
wide enough to cover two roofs at once.

Why are we so monumentally slow?
Soldiers stalk a pharmacy:
big guns, little pills.

If you tilt your head just slightly
it's ridiculous.

There's a place in this brain
where hate won't grow.
I touch its riddle: wind, and seeds.
Something pokes us as we sleep.

It's late but everything comes next.

Ducks

We thought of ourselves as people of culture.
How long will it be till others see us that way again?
IRAQI FRIEND

In her first home each book
had a light around it.
The voices of distant countries
floated in through open windows,
entering her soup and her mirror.
They slept with her in the same thick bed.

Someday she would go there.
Her voice, among all those voices.
In Iraq a book never had one owner – it had ten.
Lucky books, to be held often
and gently, by so many hands.

Later in American libraries she felt sad
for books no one ever checked out.

She lived in a country house beside a pond
and kept ducks, two male, one female.
She worried over the difficult relations
of triangles. One of the ducks
often seemed depressed.
But not the same one.

During the war between her two countries
she watched the ducks more than usual.
She stayed quiet with the ducks.
Some days they huddled among reeds
or floated together.

She could not call her family in Basra
which had grown farther away than ever
nor could they call her. For nearly a year
she would not know who was alive,
who was dead.

The ducks were building a nest.

Peace

1

People pass you in the street
and do not see you.

Apparition, hidden river,
inhabitant of cracks...

After battering talk
a room clears
and you're on the ceiling
extending your silent hand
water of light
poured freely...

a hand, not a flag.
You don't believe in flags any more.
You're not even sure
you believe in men.

Birds, children, silver trays –
no problem here.
Each day they trade their air
and song. They feed you.

2

Rounding the last old city corner to school,
for years and years
a boy touched his finger to
the same chipped stone in a wall.

Befriending one another
was no trouble.

The boy knew what came next:
tight desk, stretching hours.

Sixty years later in another country
he tells one person about the stone.

Then goes outside
to stare into trees.

Is it still there?
He will find it.
What if it is not there?
He will find it.

Stone House

My grandmother is dead
but her green trunk
must still be sitting.
Sitting in the stone room
with an arch
and a single window.
Sitting in the cool light
that touches
the chipped lid.
And I wonder where the key has gone.
The key that lived
between her breasts
whether she slept or woke.
And wouldn't let anybody touch.
I wonder if they have
emptied the trunk
or left her squares of velvet
carefully folded,
her chips of plates,
the scraps and rubble she saved
and wouldn't let us see.
Wouldn't let us see
because every life
needs a hidden place.

And I pray they
have not emptied it.

We brought her rosy soap
for the hidden place.
Heavy wedge of chocolate
twisted in foil.
She tried to eat the foil.
We brought her nothing big enough
but she saved it all.

The uncle made fun of her.
She lived too long.
The Queen of Palestine.
She would turn her face away
when he said that.
He died first.

And we never stayed.
No, we never stayed.
The trunk stayed.
The grapes shriveled in the village
and didn't come again.
This was a sadness beyond telling.
Maybe if they didn't mention it
the grapes would return.

The clay they used for jugs
also went away.
The young men
went away.
It was a hard place to be
if you were staying.

Why do I think of that key
still planted firmly in the crack
over her heart?
She used to say the stone
was smarter than people
because it never went away.

Blood

'A true Arab knows how to catch
a fly in his hands,'
my father would say. And he'd prove it,
cupping the buzzer instantly
while the host with the swatter stared.

In the spring our palms peeled.
True Arabs believed watermelon
could heal fifty ways.
I changed these to fit the occasion.

Years before, a girl knocked,
wanted to see the Arab.
I said we didn't have one.
After that, my father told more stories,
'Shihab' – 'shooting star' –
a good name, borrowed from the sky.
Once I said, 'When we die, we give it back?'
He said that's what a true Arab would say.

Today the headlines clot in my blood.
A Palestinian boy dangles a toy truck
on the front page.
Homeless fig, this tragedy with a terrible root
is too big for us. What flag can we wave?
I wave the flag of stone and seed,
table mat stitched in blue.

I call my father, we talk around the news.
It is too much for him,
neither of his two languages can reach it.
I drive into the country to find sheep, cow
to plead with the air:
Who calls anyone *civilised*?
Where can the crying heart graze?
What does a true Arab do now?

from

YOU AND YOURS

(2005)

Cross that Line

Paul Robeson stood
on the northern border
of the USA
and sang into Canada
where a vast audience
sat on folding chairs
waiting to hear him.

He sang into Canada.
His voice left the USA
when his body was
not allowed to cross
that line.

Remind us again,
brave friend.
What countries may we
sing into?
What lines should we all
be crossing?
What songs travel toward us
from far away
to deepen our days?

Someone I Love

Someone I love so much cut down my primrose patch. It looked like an oval of overgrown weeds to him, in the front yard, near the black mailbox on the post. He did not know that for weeks I had been carefully tending and watering it, as a few primroses floated their pink heads above the green mass, unfurled their delicate bonnets. With dozens of buds waiting to shine, we were on the brink, everything popping open, despite the headlines, all sweet flower beings from under the ground remembering what they were supposed to do.

He mowed it down with the old push lawn mower. I was out of town – he didn't ask his father, who knew how precious it was to me – his father was in the back while this was happening and didn't see – there wasn't a second thought – why would we have such a tall patch in the yard? – what does my mother do when she comes out here with the old shovel and the bucket and the mysterious sacks of rose food and mulch, poking around in the earth, trimming, the clippers in her pocket, bending to the wild tangle of jasmine on the fence, the Dutchman's Pipe, the happy oregano, the funny cacti crowding together in complicated profusion like a family, the miniature chiles – what does she do, why is this here?

He just cut it down. It wasn't easy.
He must have pushed really hard to get it to go.

When I stood outside in my nightie the next dreamy-sweet morning at dawn after returning home on the midnight plane, watering my bluebonnets snapdragons butterfly bush lantana, wanting to feel tied to earth again, as I always do when I get home, rooted in soil and stone and old caliche and bamboo and trees a hundred years of memory in their trunks and bushes we didn't plant, and the healthy *esperanza* never losing her hope, and the banana palms just poking out their fine and gracious greenery, when I suddenly saw what was gone, what wasn't there, not there, impossible, I was so shocked I let the hose run all over my bare feet. The cold stun of fury filled me, sorrow rising and pouring into questions, who could do this, why, how could anyone? I thought of the time my daddy came home to find every head cut off his giant sunflowers right after they had opened their faces to the sky, only the empty stalks remaining, his disbelieving sorrow as he went to his room and lay down on the bed and closed his eyes, and thought, I will not mention this, I am too sad to mention it, this is the pain of people everywhere, the pain this year deserves.

But at breakfast I went a little strange like the lady down the street who shows up at people's doors with a snarling dog and a hammer in her pocket, I went wild and furious and he swore they just looked like weeds to him, why hadn't I warned him, why did I only tell Dad?

I pointed them out to you weeks ago, I said.
He said, I don't remember flower things like that.

And it was the season of blooming and understanding. It was the season of hiding from headlines, wondering what it would do if the whole house had been erased or just the books and paintings or what about the whole reckless garden or (then it gets unthinkable but we make ourselves think it now and then to stay human) the child's arms or legs, what would I do? If I did not love him, who would I become?

Isle of Mull, Scotland

Because by now we know everything is not so green elsewhere.

The cities tied their nooses around our necks,
we let them without even seeing.

Not even feeling our breath soften
as clumps of shed wool scattered across days.

Not even. This even-ing, balance beam of light on green,
the widely lifted land, resonance of moor
winding down to water, the full of it. Days of cows
and sheep bending their heads.

We walked where the ancient pier juts into the sea.
Stood on the rim of the pool, by the circle
of black boulders. No one saw we were there
and everyone who had ever been there
stood silently in air.

Where else do we ever have to go, and why?

First Day Without You in 99 Years

Postman climbs onto creaky porch.
Not right, not right.
He didn't get the news.
Bitter leaf, bottom of cup.
No one laps it up.
Salty edge.
Where will the white coverlet migrate?
Staring at branches above curtains
day after day,
you waited to feel better,
you willed the leaves back
from their sleep.
Now what will we do?

Our Time

Robert Frost wrote 'Stopping by Woods on a Snowy Evening'
in the middle of a searing hot July.

Maybe he needed a chill, the silence
of frozen trees, to keep the air moving

in his mind. So many readers have considered
his two roads of another poem,

but maybe sweating Mr Frost invoking frost,
his secret quirky inversion, matters more.

We grew up proud of our country.
Forests of wonderful words to wander through –

freedom, indivisible.
Now my horse is lost in a sheen of lies.

The world is lovely, dark, and deep.
We honor others as they sleep.

As they wake and as they sleep.

Fresh

To move
cleanly.
Needing to be
nowhere else.
Wanting nothing
from any store.
To lift something
you already had
and set it down in
a new place.
Awakened eye
seeing freshly.
What does that do to
the old blood moving through
its channels?

The Day

I missed the day
on which it was said
others should not have
certain weapons, but we could.
Not only could, but should,
        and do.
I missed that day.
Was I sleeping?
I might have been digging
in the yard,
doing something small and slow
as usual.
Or maybe I wasn't born yet.
What about all the other people
who aren't born?
Who will tell them?

For Mohammed Zeid of Gaza, Age 15

There is no *stray* bullet, sirs.
No bullet like a worried cat
crouching under a bush,
no half-hairless puppy bullet
dodging midnight streets.
The bullet could not be a pecan
plunking tin roof,
not hardly, no fluff of pollen
on October's breath,
no humble pebble at our feet.

So don't gentle it, please.

We live among stray thoughts,
tasks abandoned midstream.
Our fickle hearts are fat
with stray devotions, we feel at home
among bits and pieces,
all the wandering ways of words.

But this bullet had no innocence, did not
wish anyone well, you can't tell us otherwise
by naming it mildly, this bullet was never the friend
of life, should not be granted immunity
by soft saying – friendly fire, straying death-eye,
why have we given the wrong weight to what we do?

Mohammed, Mohammed, deserves the truth.
This bullet had no secret happy hopes,
it was not singing to itself with eyes closed
under the bridge.

The Story, Around the Corner

is not turning the way you thought
it would turn, gently, in a little spiral loop,
the way a child draws the tail of a pig.
What came out of your mouth,
a riff of common talk.
As a sudden weather shift on a beach,
sky looming mountains of cloud
in a way you cannot predict
or guide, the story shuffles elements, darkens,
takes its own side. And it is strange.
Far more complicated than a few phrases
pieced together around a kitchen table
on a July morning in Dallas, say,
a city you don't live in, where people
might shop forever or throw a thousand stories
away. You who carried or told a tiny bit of it
aren't sure. Is this what we wanted?
Stories wandering out,
having their own free lives?
Maybe they are planning something bad.
A scrap or cell of talk you barely remember
is growing into a weird body with many demands.
One day soon it will stumble up the walk and knock,
knock hard, and you will have to answer the door.

During a War

Best wishes to you & yours,
he closes the letter.

For a moment I can't
fold it up again –
where does 'yours' end?
Dark eyes pleading
what could we have done
differently?
Your family,
your community,
circle of earth, we did not want,
we tried to stop,
we were not heard
by dark eyes who are dying
now. How easily they
would have welcomed us in
for coffee, serving it
in a simple room
with a radiant rug.
Your friends & mine.

The Sweet Arab, the Generous Arab

Since no one else is mentioning you enough.

The Arab who extends his hand.
The Arab who will not let you pass
his tiny shop without a welcoming word.
The refugee inviting us in for a Coke.
Clean glasses on a table in a ramshackle hut.
Those who don't drink Coke would drink it now.
We drink from the silver flask of hospitality.
We drink and you bow your head.

Please forgive everyone who has not honored your name.

You who would not kill a mouse, a bird.
Who feels sad sometimes even cracking an egg.
Who places two stones on top of one another
for a monument. Who packed the pieces,
carried them to a new corner. For whom the words
rubble and blast are constants. Who never wanted
those words. To be able to say,
this is a day and I live in it safely,
with those I love, was all. Who has been hurt
but never hurt in return. Fathers and grandmothers,
uncles, the little lost cousin who wanted only
to see a Ferris wheel in his lifetime, ride it
high into the air. And all the gaping days
they bought no tickets
for spinning them around.

He Said EYE-RACK

Relative to our plans for your country,
we will blast your tree, crush your cart,
stun your grocery.
Amen sisters and brothers,
give us your sesame legs,
your satchels, your skies.
Freedom will feel good
to you too. Please acknowledge
our higher purpose. No, we did not see
your bed of parsley. On St Patrick's Day
2003, President Bush wore a blue tie. Blinking hard,
he said, 'We are not dealing with peaceful men.'
He said, 'reckless aggression'.
He said, 'the danger is clear'.
Your patio was not visible in his frame.
Your comforter stuffed with wool
from a sheep you knew. He said, 'We are
against the lawless men who
rule your country, not you.' Tell that
to the mother, the sister, the bride,
the proud boy, the peanut-seller,
the librarian careful with her shelves.
The teacher, the spinner, the sweeper,
the invisible village, the thousands of people
with laundry and bread, the ants tunneling
through the dirt.

The Boy Removes All Traces from His Room

If the stuffed gray cat stares face down
into a crate forever from now on, he will not care.
Bury the cross-stitched alphabet,

the carved Russian wolf, the wooden train,
– where did all that come from anyway?
Even the pencilled height marks on the wall got

covered over by fresh paint – why keep them
when he doesn't like the lost kid with long hair anyway,
who cares how tall he wasn't?

The palette shrinks: black, white, gray.
Somewhere he saw an image of a monk's cell,
spartan clean. He will make a box for his shoes.

Wires tangle behind a desk.
Adaptors, surge protectors – defend us all.
At night he hears a weird clacking in the leaves

that might be an animal and the late train wailing
on its long way west. *Why does it make so much noise?*
Doesn't it want to go?

It is not a game, it was never a game.

It was a girl's arm, the right one
that held a pencil.
She liked her arm.

It was a small stone house
with an iron terrace,
a flower pot beside the
door.

People passing,
loaves of bread,
little plans
the size of a thought,
dropping off something you borrowed,
buying a small sack of *zaater*,
it was a hand with fingers
dipping the scoop into the barrel.

I will not live this way,
said a woman with a baby on her hip
but she was where she was.

These men do not represent me,
said the teacher with her students
in pressed blue smocks.

They had sharpened their pencils.
Desks lined in a simple room.
It was school,
numbers on a page.
a radiant sky with clouds.
In the old days you felt happy to see it.

No one wanted anything
to drop out of it
except rain. Where was rain?

It was not a game, it was
unbelievable sorrow
and fear.

A hand that a mother held.
A pocket. A glass.
It was not war.
It was people.

We had gone nowhere
in a million years.

The Light that Shines on Us Now

This strange beam of being right,
smug spotlight.
What else could we have done?
asks a little one.
What else?

Three girls with book bags
fleeing tanks.

Now that we are so bold,
now that we pretend
God likes some kinds of killing,
how will we deserve
the light of candles,
soft beam of a small lamp
falling across any safe bed?

Orphan boy in a striped shirt
trapped between two glum uncles.
He carries his mother's
smooth fragrance
and father's solid voice.
They were not countries,
they were continents.

I Feel Sorry for Jesus

People won't leave Him alone.
I know He said, *wherever two or more*
are gathered in my name...
but I'll bet some days He regrets it.

Cozily they tell you what He wants
and doesn't want
as if they just got an e-mail.
Remember 'Telephone', that pass-it-on game

where the message changed dramatically
by the time it rounded the circle?
Well.
People blame terrible pieties on Jesus.

They want to be his special pet.
Jesus deserves better.
I think He's been exhausted
for a very long time.

He went *into the desert*, friends.
He didn't go into the pomp.
He didn't go into
the golden chandeliers

and say, *the truth tastes better here.*
See? I'm talking like I know.
It's dangerous talking for Jesus.
You get carried away almost immediately.

I stood in the spot where He was born.
I closed my eyes where He died and didn't die.
Every twist of the Via Dolorosa
was written on my skin.

And that makes me feel like being silent
for Him, you know? A secret pouch
of listening. You won't hear me
mention this again.

NEW POEMS
(2008)

Ted Kooser Is My President

When I travel abroad, I will invoke
Ted's poems at checkpoints:
yes, barns, yes, memory, gentility,
the quiet little wind among stones.
If they ask, You are American?
I will say, Ted's kind of American.
No, I carry no scissors or matches.
Yes, horizons, dinner tables.
Yes, weather, the honesty of it.
Buttons, chickens. Feel free
to dump my purse. I'll wander
to the window, stare out for days.
Actually, I have never been
to Nebraska, except with Ted,
who hosted me dozens of times,
though we have never met.
His deep assurance comforts me.
He's not big on torture at all.
He could probably sneak into your country
when you weren't looking
and say something really good about it.
Have you noticed those purple blossoms
in a clump beside your wall?

The First Time I Was Old

Sky crackled
with scary lightning.
Our fuel tank had to be drained
and refilled
before the plane could fly.
What did that mean?
I said, 'Hi' to the 20-ish guy
taking the next seat.
He had bumped a woman
across the aisle
saying 'Sorry! My elbow'
so I know he spoke English.
He took one long look at me
and decidedly
didn't answer.

Land of Lincoln

And in this room
Nicholas Vachel Lindsay was born
Vachel with a V
He dropped the Nicholas
Upon editor's suggestion later
Here is the bed his mother lay in
His father's lamp
The fireplace they read by
The back door his doctor father went in and out of
They hadn't proven the germ theory yet
Which is how the Lindsay sisters
Contracted scarlet fever
The family had two bathrooms
They had so many books
These were part of their real library
This house was considered middle-class
For its time but now it seems very fine
Doesn't it? Sandburg visited here
Often and the Lincolns in earlier days would come over
For regular meals and you do recall don't you
That Vachel was the one who first introduced Langston Hughes
To the crowd where William Butler Yeats
And all the luminaries were gathered in Chicago?
Vachel went tramping out west repeatedly with no money
Only poems to trade for bread
His philosophy of beauty and simplicity in his pocket
These are copies of his drawings
He stayed in this house as a grown man too
It was his only house
The only house of a great wanderer
And he married and had children here
And it was in this room he drank the poison
That killed him

Letters My Prez Is Not Sending

Dear Rafik, Sorry about that soccer game
you won't be attending since you now
have no...

Dear Fawziya, You know, I have a mom too
so I can imagine what you...

Dear Shadiya, Think about your father
versus democracy, I'll bet you'd pick...

No, no, Sami, that's not true
what you said at the rally,
that our country hates you,
we really support your move
toward freedom,
that's why you no longer have
a house or a family or a village...

Dear Hassan, If only you could see
the bigger picture...

Dear Mary, I'm surprised you have
what we would call a Christian name
since you yourself...

Dear Ribhia, Sorry about that heart attack,
I know it must have been rough to live
your entire life under occupation,
we're sending a few more bombs over now
to fortify your oppressors,
but someday we hope for peace in the region,
sorry you won't be there to see it...

Dear Suheir, Surely a voice is made to be raised,
don't you see we are speaking
for your own interests...

Dear Sharif, Violence is wrong
unless we are using it,
why doesn't that make sense...

Dear Nadia, I did not know about
your special drawer, you know I like
to keep a few things too that have meaning to me...

Dear Ramzi, You really need to stop crying now
and go on about your business...

Dear Daddo, I know 5 kids
must feel like a lot to lose in one swoop
but we can't stop our efforts...

Dear Fatima, Of course I have feelings
for your own people, my college roommate
was from Lebanon...

Dear Mahmoud, I wish I had time
to answer your letter but you must understand
the mail has really been stacking up...

What Happened to the Air

Well there were so many currents in it after a time,
so many streams of voices crisscrossing above the high pasture
when she went out to feed the horses, gusts of ringing
and buzzing against her skin. Sometimes near the biggest live oak
she paused to feel a businessman in Waxahachie calling out
toward his office in El Paso, a mother boarding a plane in Amarillo
waking up her Comfort girl. Hard to move sometimes inside
so many longings, urgencies of time and distance,
hard to pretend everything you needed was right in front of you,
bucket and feed and fence, that bundle of hay Otto pitched inside
          your gate,
that rusting tractor Juan might fix someday. You wished everything
were still right *here*, the way it used to be,
before honeybees were in jeopardy,
when the Saturday mystery episode streaming toward your radio
was the only beam you might ride from west to east,
before we were all so strangely connected and disconnected
inside a vibrant web of signals, and a crowded wind.

Parents of Murdered Palestinian Boy
Donate His Organs to Israelis

Ahmed Ismail Khatib, you died,
but you have so many bodies now.
You became a much bigger boy.
You became a girl too –
your kidneys, your liver, your heart.
So many people needed what you had.

In a terrible moment,
your parents pressed against
spinning cycles of revenge
to do something better.
They stretched.
What can that say to the rest of us?

In the photograph your hand
is raised to your chin – position of thought.
This was not your intention.
But people you will never meet are cheering.

Please keep telling us something true.

Because of your kidneys, your liver, your heart –
we must – simply must – be bigger too.

Gate A-4

Wandering around the Albuquerque Airport Terminal, after learning my flight had been delayed four hours, I heard an announcement: 'If anyone in the vicinity of Gate A-4 understands any Arabic, please come to the gate immediately!'

Well – one pauses these days. Gate A-4 was my own gate. I went there.

An older woman in full traditional Palestinian embroidered dress, just like my grandma wore, was crumpled to the floor, wailing loudly. 'Help,' said the Flight Service Person. 'Talk to her. What is her problem? We told her the flight was going to be late and she did this.'

I stooped to put my arm around the woman and spoke to her haltingly. 'Shu-dow-a, Shu-bid-uck Habibti, Stani schway, Min fadlick, Shu-bit-se-wee?' The minute she heard any words she knew, however poorly used, she stopped crying. She thought our flight had been cancelled entirely. She needed to be in El Paso for major medical treatment the next day. I said, 'No, No, we're fine, you'll get there, just late, who is picking you up? Let's call him.'

We called her son and I spoke with him in English. I told him I would stay with his mother till we got on the plane and would ride next to her – Southwest. She talked to him. Then we called her other sons just for the fun of it. Then we called my dad and he and she spoke for a while in Arabic and found out of course they had ten shared friends. Then I thought just for the heck of it why not call some Palestinian poets I know and let them chat with her? This all took up about two hours.

She was laughing a lot by then. Telling about her life, patting my knee, answering questions. She had pulled a sack of home-made mamool cookies – little powdered sugar crumbly mounds

157

stuffed with dates and nuts – out of her bag – and was offering them to all the women at the gate. To my amazement, not a single woman declined one. It was like a sacrament. The traveler from Argentina, the mom from California, the lovely woman from Laredo – we were all covered with the same powdered sugar. And smiling. There is no better cookie.

And then the airline broke out free beverages from huge coolers and two little girls from our flight ran around serving us apple juice and they were covered with powdered sugar too. And I noticed my new best friend – by now we were holding hands – had a potted plant poking out of her bag, some medicinal thing, with green furry leaves. Such an old country traveling tradition. Always carry a plant. Always stay rooted to somewhere.

And I looked around that gate of late and weary ones and thought, This is the world I want to live in. The shared world. Not a single person in this gate – once the crying of confusion stopped – seemed apprehensive about any other person. They took the cookies. I wanted to hug all those other women too.

This can still happen anywhere. Not everything is lost.

Naomi Shihab Nye was born in 1952 in St Louis, Missouri, to a Palestinian father and an American mother of German descent. She grew up in St Louis, Jerusalem and San Antonio, Texas. Drawing on her Palestinian-American background, the cultural diversity of Texas, and her experiences in Asia, Europe, Canada, Mexico, Central and South America and the Middle East, her poetry 'reflects this textured heritage, which endowed her with an openness to the experiences of others and a sense of continuity across borders' (Bill Moyers).

She has published more than 25 books, including poetry, essays, picture books, novels and anthologies for younger readers. Her latest book of essays is *I'll Ask You Three Times, Are You Okay? Tales of Driving and Being Driven* (2007).

She has received many literary awards, and has been a Lannan Fellow, a Guggenheim Fellow, and a Witter Bynner Fellow (Library of Congress). Her work has been presented on National Public Radio on *A Prairie Home Companion* and *The Writer's Almanac*, and she has been featured on two of Bill Moyers' PBS poetry specials on American television networks. She lives in San Antonio, Texas.

Tender Spot: Selected Poems (Bloodaxe Books, 2008) is her first UK poetry publication.